The Black Christ

& OTHER POEMS

Charles Cullen

THE
BLACK CHRIST

& OTHER POEMS

By

COUNTEE CULLEN

With Decorations by
CHARLES CULLEN

Harper & Brothers Publishers

New York and London

mcmxxix

A Book
for Three Friends

EDWARD

ROBERTA

HAROLD

❦

¶ ACKNOWLEDGMENT for permission to reprint certain of these poems is made to the following magazines and collections in the pages of which they first appeared:

The Century
The New Republic
Harper's Magazine
Opportunity
The Crisis
Tambour
Ebony and Topaz
The Poetry Folio
Palms
The Archive
Time and Tide
The London Observer

¶ Grateful appreciation is also conveyed to the John Simon Guggenheim Memorial Foundation by the aid of whose grant many of these poems were written.

Contents

To the Three for Whom
the Book

ONCE like a lady
    In a silken dress,
        The serpent might eddy
Through the wilderness,
Billow and glow
And undulate
In a rustling flow
Of sinuous hate.
Now dull-eyed and leaden,
Of having lost
His Eden
He pays the cost.
He shuns the tree
That brought him low
As grown to be
Domestic; no
Temptations dapple,
From leaf to root,
The modern apple
Our meekest fruit.
Dragon and griffin
And basilisk

Whose stare could stiffen,
And the hot breath whisk
From the overbold
Braving a gaze
So freezing cold,
Who sings their praise
These latter days?
That venemous head
On a woman fair,—
Medusa's dead
Of the hissing hair.
No beasts are made
Meet for the whir
Of that sunken blade
Excalibur.
No smithies forge
A shining sword
Fit for the gorge
Of a beast abhorred.
Pale Theseus
Would have no need,
Were he with us,
Of sword or thread;
For long has been set
The baleful star
Of Pasiphaë's pet,
The Minotaur.

4

Though they are dead,
Those ancient ones,
Each bestial head
Dust under tons
Of dust, new beasts
Have come, their heirs,
Claiming their feasts
As the old did theirs.
Clawless they claw,
Fangless they rend;
And the stony maw
Crams on without end.
Still are arrayed
(But with brighter eyes)
Stripling and maid
For the sacrifice.
We cannot spare
This toll we pay
Of the slender, the fair,
The bright and the gay!
Gold and black crown,
Body slim and taut,
How they go down
'Neath the juggernaut!
Youth of the world,
Like scythèd wheat,
How they are hurled

At the clay god's feet!
Hear them cry Holy
To stone and to steel,
See them bend lowly,
Loyal and leal,
Blood rendered and bone,
To steel and to stone.
They have forgot
The stars and the sun,
The grassy plot,
And waters that run
From rock to rock;—
Their only care
Is to grasp a lock
Of Mammon's hair.

But you three rare
Friends whom I love
(With rhymes to swear
The depths whereof)
A book to you three
Who have not bent
The idolatrous knee,
Nor worship lent
To modern rites,
Knowing full well
How a just god smites

The infidel;
Three to whom Pan
Is no mere myth,
But a singing Man
To be reckoned with;—
Witness him now
In the mist and dew;
Lean and hear how
He carols to you:
"Gather as a flower
Living to your heart;
Let the full shower
Rankle and smart;
Youth is the coffer
Where all is hid;
All age may offer
Youth can outbid.
Blind with your beauty
The ranks of scorn,
Take for a duty
Pleasure; you were born
Joy to incur.
Ere the eyes are misted
With a rheumy blur,
Ere the speech is twisted
To a throaty slur,
Ere the cheeks are haggard;

7

Ere the prick of the spur
Finds you lame or laggard,
Do not demur!
When Time advances
Terrible and lone,
Recall there were dances
Though they be flown.
When Death plys the riddle
To which all are mute,
Remember the fiddle,
The lyre and the flute."

To three who will heed
His song, nor brook
That a god should plead
In vain, a book.

Tribute

(To My Mother)

BECAUSE man is not virtuous in him-
    self,
    Nor kind, nor given to sweet charities,
Save goaded by the little kindling elf
Of some dear face it pleasures him to please;
Some men who else were humbled to the dust,
Have marveled that the chastening hand
    should stay,
And never dreamed they held their lives in
    trust
To one the victor loved a world away.
So I, least noble of a churlish race,
Least kind of those by nature rough and
    crude,
Have at the intervention of your face
Spared him with whom was my most bitter
    feud
One moment, and the next, a deed more
    grand,
The helpless fly imprisoned in my hand.

That Bright Chimeric Beast

(For Lynn Riggs)

THAT bright chimeric beast
    Conceived yet never born,
    Save in the poet's breast,
The white-flanked unicorn,
Never may be shaken
From his solitude;
Never may be taken
In any earthly wood.

That bird forever feathered,
Of its new self the sire,
After aeons weathered,
Reincarnate by fire,
Falcon may not nor eagle
Swerve from his eerie,
Nor any crumb inveigle
Down to an earthly tree.

That fish of the dread regime
Invented to become
The fable and the dream
Of the Lord's aquarium,
Leviathan, the jointed

Harpoon was never wrought
By which the Lord's anointed
Will suffer to be caught.

Bird of the deathless breast,
Fish of the frantic fin,
That bright chimeric beast
Flashing the argent skin,—
If beasts like these you'd harry,
Plumb then the poet's dream;
Make it your aviary,
Make it your wood and stream.
There only shall the swish
Be heard, of the regal fish;
There like a golden knife
Dart the feet of the unicorn,
And there, death brought to life,
The dead bird be reborn.

At the Etoile

(At the Unknown Soldier's Grave in Paris)

IF IN the lists of life he bore him well,
   Sat gracefully or fell unhorsed in love,
   No tongue is dowered now with speech to
     tell
Since he and death somewhere matched glove
     with glove.

What proud or humble union gave him birth,
Not reckoning on this immortal bed,
Is one more riddle that the cryptic earth
Though knowing chooses to retain unsaid.

Since he was weak as other men,—or like
Young Galahad as fair in thought as limb,
Each bit of moving dust in France may strike
Its breast in pride, knowing he stands for
     him.

Two Epitaphs

1 For the Unknown Soldier (Paris)

UNKNOWN but not unhonored rest,
Symbol of all Time shall not reap;
Not one stilled heart in that torn breast,
But a myriad millions sleep.

2 For a Child Still-born

HERE sleeps a spark that never burned,
A seed not granted spring to bloom,
A soul whose darkened pathway turned
From tomb of flesh to dusty tomb.

To an Unknown Poet

L OVE is enough," I read somewhere;
    Lines some poor poet in his pride
    And poverty wrote on the air
To ease his heart, and soothe his bride.

Something in me, child of an age
Cold to the core, undeified,
Warmed to my brother bard, this sage;
And I too leaned upon my pride.

But pride I found can blind our eyes,
And poverty is worse than pride.
Love's breed from both is a nest of lies;
And singer of sweet songs, you lied.

Little Sonnet to Little Friends

LET not the proud of heart condemn
   Me that I mould my ways to hers,
   Groping for healing in a hem
No wind of passion ever stirs;
Nor let them sweetly pity me
When I am out of sound and sight;
They waste their time and energy;
No mares encumber me at night.

Always a trifle fond and strange,
And some have said a bit bizarre,
Say, "Here's the sun," I would not change
It for my dead and burnt-out star.
Shine as it will, I have no doubt
Some day the sun, too, may go out.

Mood

I THINK an impulse stronger than my
    mind
    May some day grasp a knife, unloose a
    vial,
Or with a little leaden ball unbind
The cords that tie me to the rank and file.
My hands grow quarrelsome with bitterness,
And darkly bent upon the final fray;
Night with its stars upon a grave seems less
Indecent than the too complacent day.

God knows I would be kind, let live, speak
    fair,
Requite an honest debt with more than just,
And love for Christ's dear sake these shapes
    that wear
A pride that had its genesis in dust,—
The meek are promised much in a book I
    know
But one grows weary turning cheek to blow.

Counter Mood

LET this be scattered far and wide, laid
  low
  Upon the waters as they fall and rise,
Be caught and carried by the winds that blow,
Nor let it be arrested by the skies:
I who am mortal say I shall not die;
I who am dust of this am positive,
That though my nights tend toward the grave,
  yet I
Shall on some brighter day arise, and live.

Ask me not how I am oracular,
Nor whence this arrogant assurance springs.
Ask rather Faith the canny conjurer,
(Who while your reason mocks him mystifies
Winning the grudging plaudits of your
  eyes)—
How suddenly the supine egg has wings.

The Wind and the Weather

FOREVER shall not burn his tongue
    So glibly after this;
   Eternity was brief that hung
Upon a passing kiss.

A year ago no metaphor
   Was rich enough to trace
A single figure boasting more
   Allurement than her face.

One spring from then, small change we find
   In him; she still is fair.
But in the other's heart or mind
   Neither glows anywhere.

In the Midst of Life

BUD bursting from a tomb
    Of dust, this mortal knows
    In winter's sterile womb
For your despoiling grows
What comes to every rose.

Grass so securely green,
Sky-climbing corn so tall,
Know in your length is seen
What overtowers all:
The shadow of the fall.

Yet blossoms with each spring
Reopen; grasses sprout;
And jaunty corn stalks fling
New skeins of silk about.
Nature is skilled to rout

Death's every ambuscade;
For man alone is poured
The potion once essayed
That sharper than a sword
Destroys both mouth and gourd.

Deplore, lament, bewail;
The sword seeks out the sheath;
Though all things else may fail,
Two things keep faith; this breath
A while; and longer death.

Minutely Hurt

SINCE I was minutely hurt,
   Giant griefs and woes
   Only find me staunchly girt
Against all other blows.

Once an atom cracks the heart
All is done and said;
Poison, steel, and fiery dart
May then be buffeted.

Never the Final Stone

THOUGH by the glory of your lady's face
The riots of the sun and moon are quelled,
Yet have the hands that fashioned her some grace
Whereto perfection was allied, withheld.

The perfect wooer never speaks the word
The object of his passion most would hear;
So does expectance keep her wild feet spurred
Toward that which ever is no more than near.

And daily from His lonely mountain-top,
God sees us rear our Babels on the plain;
Then with one stone to go, He lets us drop
That we may want and strive for Him again.

Light Lady

THEY say when virtue slipped from her,
 Awakened by her fall,
 Sin seemed to work a miracle
And made her soul grow tall.

Here with her penny papers by,
We see how well she diced:
Nothing to do but munch her gums
And sing the love of Christ.

And now with alms for what she was
Men stroke her ragged fur;
When Death comes down this street, his face
Will not be strange to her.

24

By Their Fruits

I KNOW a lover when I see one,
   And I can tell the way they fare:
   If those they dote on shed some sun,
Or blow a cool and languid air.

Those that are loved, though niggardly,
Move with a lively foot and eye;
The others drag like men who see
Their day and minute set to die.

A Miracle Demanded

THIS life is like a tree that flourisheth
 With fruit and flower, gay leaf and
 sprouting twig;
But pestilence is in the wind's warm breath,
And at the roots the worms and mice grow
 big.
The gardener, steady in his anxious claims,
Who prunes for love, he says, and not for
 wage,
Than simple care has more disastrous names,
The most elect: Disease, Death, and Old Age.

Against such foes how shall a tree prevail
To curb its consummation in decay,
And like a tree shall men not strive and fail,
Unless all wonders have not passed away?
Renew an ancient vision, Lord, in me:
Open the young man's eyes that he may see.

Tongue-tied

YOU ask me why I love her, and you pause
   Magnanimous, that I may make reply
   Handing you deftly parceled every
   cause,
Saying with confidence, "Lo, this is why."
But I am mute as if I had no tongue,
Without reason as if I had no mind,
This song the most familiar ever sung,
Is lost to me like a leaf caught in the wind.

And so my tongue is tied; and so you smile
Not knowing, little lover that you are,
(Prattling, " 'Twill wear, 'twill last so long
   a while")
The poet is compelled to love his star,
Not knowing he could never tell you why
Though silence makes inadequate reply.

Ultima Verba

NOT being in my coffin, yet I know
    What suffocations crowd their breath
  who go
Through some mischance alive into the
    grave;
Not having any wound at all to shout
Belief to Thomas who must see or doubt,
I feel my life blood ebbing wave on wave.

And yet this knowledge cannot summon
    strength
To rend apart the life-impaling length
Of these strong boards that hold my body
    down;
There is no cloth, no cool and radiant stuff
(Save fashioned by your hand) healing
    enough
To staunch this thin red flow in which I
    drown.

I am as one knowing what day he dies,
Who looks in vain for mercy into eyes
No glints of pity shade, no pardons stir,

And thinks, "Although the trap by which I
    span
This world and that another springs, this man
Is both my judge and executioner."

The Foolish Heart

BE STILL, heart, cease those measured
      strokes;
  Lie quiet in your hollow bed;
This moving frame is but a hoax
To make you think you are not dead."

Thus spake I to my body's slave,
With beats still to be answerèd;
Poor foolish heart that needs a grave
To prove to it that it is dead.

A Wish

I HOPE when I have sung my rounds
   Of song, I shall have strength to slay
   The wish to chirp on any grounds,
Content that silence hold her sway,
My tongue not rolling futile sounds
After my heart has had its say.

For Helen Keller

AGAINST our puny sound and sight
  In vain the bells of Heaven ring,
  The Mystic Blossoms red and white
May not intrigue our visioning.

For lest we handle, lest we touch,
Lest carnally our minds condone,
Our clumsy credence may not clutch
The under or the overtone.

Her finer alchemy converts
The clanging brass to golden-pealed,
And for her sight the black earth spurts
Hues never thought there unrevealed.

Asked and Answered

HOW have I found this favor in your sight,
    And will the flame burn steady to the
end,
Until we pass that dark and dangerous bend
Where there is such a crying need for light;
Or will it flare up now, flame-clear and
    bright,
Sun-like its wealth so far and wide distend
That nothing will remain for us to spend
When toll is taken of the dismal night?

Why should I harrow up my mind like this
To tarnish with a doubt each golden kiss?
This is the Day most certainly. This bars
Us now from any hidden darkness spun.
Sufficient to the day let be the sun,
And to the night the spear-points of the stars.

Two Poets

"THE love-mad lark you sing of swooned,"
    they said,
    "And speared his bosom on a thorn of
last
Year's rose; cease playing Orpheus; no blast
You blow can raise Eurydice once dead.
Our ears are cloyed with songs our fathers
    heard
Of how your lady's face and form were fair;
Put by your fluting; swell a martial air,
And spur us on with some prophetic word."

So, wearying, he changed his tune, and won
The praise of little men (who needed
    none) . . .
But oh to see him smile as when dawn blew
A trumpet only he could hear, and dew
He could not brush away besieged his eyes
At sight of gulls departing from his skies.

H OW could a woman love him; love, or
       wed?"
    And thinking only of his tuneless face
And arms that held no hint of skill or grace,
They shook a slow, commiserative head
To see him amble by; but still they fed
Their wilting hearts on his, were fired to race
Once more, and panting at life's deadly pace,
They drank as wine the blood-in-song he
    shed.

Yet in the dream-walled room where last he
    lay,
Soft garments gathered dust all night and
    day,
As women whom he loved and sang of came
To smooth his brow and wail a secret name.
A rose placed in his hand by Guinevere
Was drenched with Magdalen's eternal tear.

Not Sacco and Vanzetti

THESE men who do not die, but send to
       death,
   These iron men whom mercy cannot
bend
Beyond the lettered law; what when their
breath
Shall suddenly and naturally end?
What shall their final retribution be,
What bloody silver then shall pay the tolls
Exacted for this legal infamy
When death indicts their stark immortal
souls?

The day a slumbering but awful God,
Before Time to Eternity is blown,
Examines with the same unyielding rod
These images of His with hearts of stone,
These men who do not die, but death de-
cree,—
These are the men I should not care to be.

A Song No Gentleman
Would Sing to Any Lady

THERE were some things I might not know
        Had you not pedagogued me so;
And these I thank you for;
Now never shall a piquant face
Cause my tutored heart a trace
Of anguish any more.

Before your pleasure made me wise
A simulacrum of disguise
Masked the serpent and the dove;
That I discern now hiss from coo,
My heart's full gratitude to you,
Lady I had learned to love.

Before I knew love well I sang
Many a polished pain and pang
With proper bardic zeal;
But now I know hearts do not break
So easily, and though a snake
Has made them, wounds may heal.

Self Criticism

SHALL I go all my bright days singing,
    (A little pallid, a trifle wan)
        The failing note still vainly clinging
To the throat of the stricken swan?

Shall I never feel and meet the urge
To bugle out beyond my sense
That the fittest song of earth is a dirge,
And only fools trust Providence?

Than this better the reed never turned flute,
Better than this no song,
Better a stony silence, better a mute
Mouth and a cloven tongue.

A Thorn Forever in the Breast

A HUNGRY cancer will not let him rest
Whose heart is loyal to the least of
dreams;
There is a thorn forever in his breast
Who cannot take his world for what it seems;
Aloof and lonely must he ever walk,
Plying a strange and unaccustomed tongue,
An alien to the daily round of talk,
Mute when the sordid songs of earth are sung.

This is the certain end his dream achieves:
He sweats his blood and prayers while others
        sleep,
And shoulders his own coffin up a steep
Immortal mountain, there to meet his doom
Between two wretched dying men, of whom
One doubts, and one for pity's sake believes.

The Proud Heart

THAT lively organ, palpitant and red,
    Enrubied in the staid and sober breast,
    Telling the living man, "You are not
    dead
Until this hammered anvil takes its rest,"
My life's timepiece wound to alarm some day
The body to its need of box and shroud,
Was meant till then to beat one haughty way;
A crimson stroke should be no less than
    proud.

Yet this high citadel has come to grief,
Been broken as an arrow drops its bird,
Splintered as many ways as veins in a leaf
At a woman's laugh or a man's harsh word;
But being proud still strikes its hours in pain;
The dead man lives, and none perceives him
    slain.

Interlude

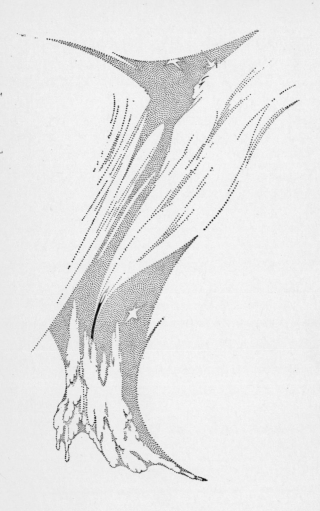

The Simple Truth

I KNOW of all the words I speak or write,
Precious and woven of a vibrant sound,
None ever snares your faith, intrigues you
  quite,
Or sends you soaring from the solid ground.
You are the level-headed lover who
Can match my fever while the kisses last,
But you are never shaken through and
  through;
Your roots are firm after the storm has passed.

I shall know nights of tossing in my sleep
Fondling a hollow where a head should lie;
But you a calm review, no tears to weep,
No wounds to dress, no futile breaths to sigh.
Ever this was the way of wind with flame:
To harry it, then leave swift as it came.

Therefore, Adieu

NOW you are gone, and with your un-
    returning goes
All I had thought in spite of you would stay;
Now draws forever to its unawakening close
The beauty of the bright bandanna'd day.

Now sift in ombrous flakes and revolutions
    slow
My dreams descending from my heady sky.
The balm I kept to cool my grief in (leaves
    of snow)
Now melts, with your departure flowing by.

I knew, indeed, the straight unswerving track
    the sun
Took to your face (as other ecstasies)
Yet I had thought some faith to me in them;
    they run
From me to you as fly to honey, bees.

Avid, to leave me neither fevered joy nor
    ache,
Only of soul and body vast unrest.

Sun, moon, and stars should be enough; why
    must you take
The feeling of the heart out of the breast?

Now I who dreamed before I died to shoot
    one shaft
Of courage from a warped and crooked bow,
Stand utterly forsaken, stripped of that small
    craft
I had, watching with you all prowess go.

At a Parting

LET us not turn for this aside to die,
  Crying a lover may not be a friend.
Our grief is vast enough without that lie;
All stories may not boast a happy end.
Love was a flower, sweet, and flowers fade;
Love was a fairy tale; these have their close.
The endless chronicle was never made,
Nor, save in dreams, the ever-scented rose.

Seeing them dim in passion's diadem,
Our rubies that were bright that now are dull,
Let them not fade without their requiem,
How they were red one time and beautiful,
And how the heart where once a ruby bled
May live, yet bear that mark till it is dead.

Dictum

YEA, I have put thee from me utterly,
  And they who plead thy cause do plead
  in vain;
Window and door are bolted, never key
From any ore shall cozen them again.
This is my regal justice: banishment,
That those who please me now may read and
      see
How self-sustained I am, with what content
I thrive alike on love or treachery.

God, Thou hast Christ, they say, at Thy right
      hand;
Close by Thy left Michael is straight and
      leal;
Around Thy throne the chanting elders stand,
And on the earth Thy feudal millions kneel.
Criest Thou never, Lord, above their song:
"But Lucifer was tall, his wings were long?"

Revelation

PITY me, I said;
   But you cried, Pity you;
And suddenly I saw
Higher than my own grief grew.
I saw a tree of woe so tall,
So deeply boughed with grief,
That matched with it my bitter plant
Was dwarfed into a leaf.

Bright Bindings

YOUR love to me was like an unread book,
  Bright-backed, with smooth white pages
  yet unslit;
Fondly as a lover, foolishly, I took
It from its shelf one day and opened it.
Here shall I read, I thought, beauty and
    grace,
The soul's most high and awful poetry:—
Alas for lovers and the faith they place
In love, alas for you, alas for me.

I have but read a page or two at most,
The most my horror-blinded eyes may read.
I find here but a windy tapering ghost
Where I sought flesh gifted to ache and bleed.
Yet back you go, though counterfeit you be.
I love bright books even when they fail me.

Ghosts

BREAST under breast when you shall lie
    With him who in my place
Bends over you with flashing eye
    And ever nearing face;

Hand fast in hand when you shall tread
    With him the springing ways
Of love from me inherited
    After my little phase;

Be not surprised if suddenly
    The couch or air confound
Your ravished ears upbraidingly,
    And silence turn to sound.

But never let it trouble you,
    Or cost you one caress;
Ghosts are soon sent with a word or two
    Back to their loneliness.

Song in Spite of Myself

NEVER love with all your heart,
    It only ends in aching;
And bit by bit to the smallest part
    That organ will be breaking.

Never love with all your mind,
    It only ends in fretting;
In musing on sweet joys behind,
    Too poignant for forgetting.

Never love with all your soul,
    For such there is no ending,
Though a mind that frets may find control,
    And a shattered heart find mending.

Give but a grain of the heart's rich seed,
    Confine some under cover,
And when love goes, bid him God-speed.
    And find another lover.

Nothing Endures

NOTHING endures,
   Not even love,
Though the warm heart purrs
Of the length thereof.

Though beauty wax,
Yet shall it wane;
Time lays a tax
On the subtlest brain.

Let the blood riot,
Give it its will;
It shall grow quiet,
It shall grow still.

Nirvana gapes
For all things given;
Nothing escapes,
Love not even.

There Must Be Words

THIS wound will be effaced as others
      have,
  This scar recede into oblivion,
Leaving the skin immaculate and suave,
With none to guess the thing they gaze upon.
After a decent show of mourning I,
As once I ever was, shall be as free
To look on love with calm unfaltering eye,
And marvel that such fools as lovers be.

These are brave words from one who like a
      child
Cuts dazzling arabesques on summer ice
That, kissed by sun, begins to crack and thaw;
The old assurance dies, only the wild
Desire to live goes on; any device
Compels its frantic grasp, even a straw.

One Day I Told My Love

ONE day I told my love my heart,
  Disclosed it out and in;
I let her read the ill-writ chart
Small with virtue, big with sin.

I took it from the hidden socket
  Where it was wont to grieve;
"I'll turn it," I said, "into a locket,
  Or a bright band for your sleeve."

I let her hold the naked thing
  No one had seen before;
And had she willed, her hand might wring
  It dry and drop it to the floor.

It was a gentle thing she did,
  The wisest and the best;
"The proper place for a heart," she said,
  "Is back in the sheltering breast."

Lesson

I LAY in silence at her side,
  My heart's and spirit's choice;
    For we had said harsh things and cried
  On love in a bitter voice.

We lay and watched two points in space,
  Pricked in heaven, faint and far.
They seemed so near, but who could trace
  That width between star and star?

We lay and watched, and suddenly
  There was a streak of light,
And where were two, the eye might see
  But one star in the night.

My hand stole out, her hand crept near,
  Grief was a splintered spar;
Two fused in one there, did you hear
  Us claiming kinship, star?

The Street Called Crooked

(Le Havre, August 1928)

"*BON soir, monsieur,*" they called to me;
  And, "*Venez voir nos femmes.*"
"*Bon soir, mesdames,*" they got from me,
  And, "*J'ai une meilleure dame.*"

"To meet strange lips and foreign eyes
  I did not cross the foam,
I have a dearer, fairer prize
  Who waits for me at home."

"Her eyes are browner, lips more red
  Than any lady's light;
'Twould grieve her heart and droop her head
  If I failed her tonight."

"*Bon soir, mesdames; que Dieu vous garde;*
  And catch this coin I throw;
The ways of life are bleak and hard,
  Ladies, I think you know."

A bright and crooked street it gleamed
  With light and laughter filled;
All night the warm wine frothed and streamed
  While souls were stripped and killed.

The Law That Changeth Not

STERN legislation of a Persian hand
   Upon my heart, Love, strict Medean
     writ,
Must till the end of time and me command
Obeisance from him who fostered it.
All other codes may hide their littlest flaw
Toward which the hopeful prisoner may
     kneel;
I come of those who once they write a law
Do barricade themselves against appeal.

So stand I now condemned by mine own tort;
Extenuations? There is none to plead.
I am my own most ultimate resort;
There is no pardon for the stricken Mede.
I turn to go, half valiant, half absurd,
To perish on a promise, die on a word.

Valedictory

NO WORD upon the boarded page
    That once in praise I spoke,
Would I in bitterness and rage,
Had I the power, revoke.
Take them and bind them to your heart,
With ribbon or with rue.
An end arrives to all we start;
I write no more of you.

Go then, adhere to the vows you make
Out of a haughty heart;
No more to tremble for my sake
Nor writhe beneath the smart
Of hearing on an alien tongue
Tolled lightly and in play,
The bell by which our lives were rung,
The bell we break today.

Love ever was the brightest dream
My pen might seize upon;
Think not I shall renounce the theme
Now that the dream is done.

We are put by, but not the Bow,
The Arrows, and the Dove.
Though you and I go down, still glow
The armaments of love.

The essence shines devoid of form,
Passion plucked of its sting,
The Holy Rose that hides no worm,
The Everlasting Thing.
Though loud I cry on Venus' name
To heal me and subdue
The rising tide, the raging flame,
I write no more of you.

Rare was the poem we began
(We called it that!) to live,
And for a while the measures ran
With all the heart could give.
But, oh, the golden vein was thin,
Early the dark cock crew;
The heart cried out (love's muezzin):
I write no more of you.

Color

To Certain Critics

THEN call me traitor if you must,
  Shout treason and default!
Say I betray a sacred trust
Aching beyond this vault.
I'll bear your censure as your praise,
For never shall the clan
Confine my singing to its ways
Beyond the ways of man.

No racial option narrows grief,
Pain is no patriot,
And sorrow plaits her dismal leaf
For all as lief as not.
With blind sheep groping every hill,
Searching an oriflamme,
How shall the shepherd heart then thrill
To only the darker lamb?

Black Majesty

(After reading John W. Vandercook's
chronicle of sable glory)

THESE men were kings, albeit they were
      black,
Christophe and Dessalines and L'Ouverture;
Their majesty has made me turn my back
Upon a plaint I once shaped to endure.
These men were black, I say, but they were
      crowned
And purple-clad, however brief their time.
Stifle your agony; let grief be drowned;
We know joy had a day once and a clime.

Dark gutter-snipe, black sprawler-in-the-
      mud,
A thing men did a man may do again.
What answer filters through your sluggish
      blood
To these dark ghosts who knew so bright a
      reign?
"Lo, I am dark, but comely," Sheba sings.
"And we were black," three shades reply,
      "but kings."

Song of Praise

WHO lies with his milk-white maiden,
    Bound in the length of her pale gold
       hair,
Cooled by her lips with the cold kiss laden,
He lies, but he loves not there.

Who lies with his nut-brown maiden,
Bruised to the bone by her sin-black hair,
Warmed with the wine that her full lips trade
    in,
He lies, and his love lies there.

The Black Christ

(*Hopefully dedicated to White America*)

The Black Christ

GOD'S glory and my country's shame,
    And how one man who cursed Christ's
       name
May never fully expiate
That crime till at the Blessed Gate
Of Heaven He meet and pardon me
Out of His love and charity;
How God, who needs no man's applause,
For love of my stark soul, of flaws
Composed, seeing it slip, did stoop
Down to the mire and pick me up,
And in the hollow of His hand
Enact again at my command
The world's supremest tragedy,
Until I die my burthen be;
How Calvary in Palestine,
Extending down to me and mine,
Was but the first leaf in a line
Of trees on which a Man should swing
World without end, in suffering
For all men's healing, let me sing.

O world grown indolent and crass,
I stand upon your bleak morass
Of incredulity and cry
Your lack of faith is but a lie.
If you but brushed the scales apart
That cloud your eyes and clinch your heart
There is no telling what grace might
Be leveled to your clearer sight;
Nor what stupendous choir break
Upon your soul till you should ache
(If you but let your fingers veer,
And raised to heaven a listening ear)
In utter pain in every limb
To know and sing as they that hymn.
If men would set their lips to prayer
With that delight with which they swear,
Heaven and earth as bow and string,
Would meet, would be attuned and sing.

We are diseased, trunk, branch, and shoot;
A sickness gathers at the root
Of us. We flaunt a gaudy fruit
But maggots wrangle at the core.
We cry for angels; yet wherefore,
Who raise no Jacobs any more? . . .
No men with eyes quick to perceive
The Shining Thing, clutch at its sleeve,

Against the strength of Heaven try
The valiant force of men who die;—
With heaving heart where courage sings
Strive with a mist of Light and Wings,
And wrestle all night long, though pressed
Be rib to rib and back to breast,
Till in the end the lofty guest
Pant, "Conquering human, be thou blest."

As once they stood white-plumed and still,
All unobserved on Dothan's hill,
Now, too, the angels, stride for stride,
Would march with us, but are denied.
Did we but let our credence sprout
As we do mockery and doubt,
Lord Christ Himself would stand revealed
In every barren, frosty field
That we misname the heart. Belief
In something more than pain and grief,
In only earth's most commonplace,
Might yet illumine every face
Of wretchedness, every blinded eye,
If from the hermitage where nigh
These thousand years the world of men
Has hemmed her in, might come again
With gracious eyes and gentle breath
The still unconquered Lady, Faith.

Two brothers have I had on earth,
One of spirit, one of sod;
My mother suckled one at birth,
One was the Son of God.

Since that befell which came to me,
Since I was singled out to be,
Upon a wheel of mockery,
The pattern of a new faith spun;
I never doubt that once the sun
For respite stopped in Gibeon,
Or that a Man I could not know
Two thousand ageless years ago,
To shape my profit by His loss,
Bought my redemption on a cross.

2

"Now spring that heals the wounds of earth
Is being born; and in her birth
The wounds of men may find a cure.
By such a thought I may endure,
And of some things be no less sure.
This is a cruel land, this South,
And bitter words to twist my mouth,
Burning my tongue down to its root,
Were easily found; but I am mute

Before the wonder of this thing:
That God should send so pure a spring,
Such grass to grow, such birds to sing,
And such small trees bravely to sprout
With timid leaves first coming out.
A land spring yearly levies on
Is gifted with God's benison.
The very odor of the loam
Fetters me here to this, my home.
The whitest lady in the town
Yonder trailing a silken gown
Is less kin to this dirt than I.
Rich mistresses with proud heads high
This dirt and I are one to them;
They flick us both from the bordered hem
Of lovely garments we supply;
But I and the dirt see just as high
As any lady cantering by.
Why should I cut this bond, my son,
This tie too taut to be undone?
This ground and I are we not one?
Has it not birthed and grown and fed me:
Yea, if you will, and also bled me?
That little patch of wizened corn
Aching and straining to be born,
May render back at some small rate
The blood and bone of me it ate.

The weevil there that rends apart
My cotton also tears my heart.
Here too, your father, lean and black,
Paid court to me with all the knack
Of any dandy in the town,
And here were born, and here have grown,
His sons and mine, as lean and black.
What ghosts there are in this old shack
Of births and deaths, soft times and hard!
I count it little being barred
From those who undervalue me.
I have my own soul's ecstasy.
Men may not bind the summer sea,
Nor set a limit to the stars;
The sun seeps through all iron bars;
The moon is ever manifest.
These things my heart always possessed.
And more than this (and here's the crown)
No man, my son, can batter down
The star-flung ramparts of the mind.
So much for flesh; I am resigned,
Whom God has made shall He not guide?"

So spake my mother, and her pride
For one small minute in its tide
Bore all my bitterness away.
I saw the thin bent form, the gray

Hair shadowed in the candlelight,
The eyes fast parting with their sight,
The rough, brown fingers, lean with toil,

Marking her kinship to the soil.
Year crowding year, after the death
Of that one man whose last drawn breath
Had been the gasping of her name,

75

She had wrought on, lit with some flame
Her children sensed, but could not see,
And with a patient wizardry
Wheedled her stubborn bit of land
To yield beneath her coaxing hand,
And sometimes in a lavish hour
To blossom even with a flower.
Time after time her eyes grew dim
Watching a life pay for the whim
Some master of the land must feed
To keep her people down. The seed
They planted in her children's breasts
Of hatred toward these men like beasts
She weeded out with legends how
Once there had been somewhere as now
A people harried, low in the dust;
But such had been their utter trust
In Heaven and its field of stars
That they had broken down their bars,
And walked across a parted sea
Praising His name who set them free.
I think more than the tales she told,
The music in her voice, the gold
And mellow notes she wrought,
Made us forbear to voice the thought
Low-buried underneath our love,
That we saw things she knew not of.

We had no scales upon our eyes;
God, if He was, kept to His skies,
And left us to our enemies.
Often at night fresh from our knees
And sorely doubted litanies
We grappled for the mysteries:
"We never seem to reach nowhere,"
Jim with a puzzled, questioning air,
Would kick the covers back and stare
For me the elder to explain.
As like as not, my sole refrain
Would be, "A man was lynched last night."
"Why?" Jim would ask, his eyes star-bright.
"A white man struck him; he showed fight.
Maybe God thinks such things are right."
"Maybe God never thinks at all—
Of us," and Jim would clench his small,
Hard fingers tight into a ball.

"Likely there ain't no God at all,"
Jim was the first to clothe a doubt
With words, that long had tried to sprout
Against our wills and love of one
Whose faith was like a blazing sun
Set in a dark, rebellious sky.
Now then the roots were fast, and I

Must nurture them in her despite.
God could not be, if He deemed right,
The grief that ever met our sight.

Jim grew; a brooder, silent, sheathed;
But pride was in the air he breathed;
Inside you knew an Ætna seethed.
Often when some new holocaust
Had come to undermine and blast
The life of some poor wretch we knew,
His bones would show like white scars
    through
His fists in anger's futile way.
"I have a fear," he used to say,
"This thing may come to me some day.
Some man contemptuous of my race
And its lost rights in this hard place,
Will strike me down for being black.
But when I answer I'll pay back
The late revenge long overdue
A thousand of my kind and hue.
A thousand black men, long since gone
Will guide my hand, stiffen the brawn,
And speed one life-divesting blow
Into some granite face of snow.
And I may swing, but not before
I send some pale ambassador

Hot footing it to hell to say
A proud black man is on his way."

When such hot venom curled his lips
And anger snapped like sudden whips
Of lightning in his eyes, her words,—
Slow, gentle as the fall of birds
That having strained to win aloft
Spread out their wings and slowly waft
Regretfully back to the earth,—
Would challenge him to name the worth
Contained in any seed of hate.
Ever the same soft words would mate
Upon her lips: love, trust, and wait.
But he, young, quick, and passionate,
Could not so readily conceal,
Deeper than acid-burns, or steel
Inflicted wounds, his vital hurt;
So still the bitter phrase would spurt:
"The things I've seen, the things I see,
Show what my neighbor thinks of me.
The world is large enough for two
Men any time, of any hue.
I give pale men a wide berth ever;
Best not to meet them, for I never
Could bend my spirit, never truckle
To them; my blood's too hot to knuckle."

And true; the neighbors spoke of him
As that proud nigger, handsome Jim.
It was a grudging compliment,
Half paid in jest, half fair intent,
By those whose partial, jaundiced eye
Saw each of us as one more fly,
Or one more bug the summer brings,
All shaped alike; antennæ, wings,
And noxious all; if caught, to die.
But Jim was not just one more fly,
For he was handsome in a way
Night is after a long, hot day.
If blood flows on from heart to heart,
And strong men leave their counterpart
In vice and virtue in their seed,
Jim's bearing spoke his imperial breed.
I was an offshoot, crude, inclined
More to the earth; he was the kind
Whose every graceful movement said,
As blood must say, by turn of head,
By twist of wrist, and glance of eye,
"Good blood flows here, and it runs high."
He had an ease of limb, a raw,
Clean, hilly stride that women saw
With quickened throbbings of the breast.
There was a show of wings; the nest
Was too confined; Jim needed space

To loop and dip and interlace;
For he had passed the stripling stage,
And stood a man, ripe for the wage
A man extorts of life; his gage
Was down. The beauty of the year
Was on him now, and somewhere near
By in the woods, as like as not,
His cares were laid away, forgot
In hearty wonderment and praise
Of one of spring's all perfect days.

But in my heart a shadow walked
At beauty's side; a terror stalked
For prey this loveliness of time.
A curse lay on this land and clime.
For all my mother's love of it,
Prosperity could not be writ
In any book of destiny
For this most red epitome
Of man's consistent cruelty
To man. Corruption, blight, and rust
Were its reward, and canker must
Set in. There were too many ghosts
Upon its lanes, too many hosts
Of dangling bodies in the wind,
Too many voices, choked and thinned,
Beseeching mercy on its air.

And like the sea set in my ear
Ever there surged the steady fear
Lest this same end and brutal fate
March toward my proud, importunate
Young brother. Often he'd say,
" 'Twere best, I think, we moved away."
But custom and an unseen hand
Compelled allegiance to this land
In her, and she by staying nailed
Us there, by love securely jailed.

But love and fear must end their bout,
And one or both be counted out.
Rebellion barked now like a gun;
Like a split dam, this faith in one
Who in my sight had never done
One extraordinary thing
That I should praise his name, or sing
His bounty and his grace, let loose
The pent-up torrent of abuse
That clamored in me for release:
"Nay, I have done with deities
Who keep me ever on my knees,
My mouth forever in a tune
Of praise, yet never grant the boon
Of what I pray for night and day.
God is a toy; put Him away.

Or make you one of wood or stone
That you can call your very own,
A thing to feel and touch and stroke,
Who does not break you with a yoke
Of iron that he whispers soft;
Nor promise you fine things aloft
While back and belly here go bare,
While His own image walks so spare
And finds this life so hard to live
You doubt that He has aught to give.
Better an idol shaped of clay
Near you, than one so far away.
Although it may not heed your labors,
At least it will not mind your neighbors'.
'In His own time, He will unfold
You milk and honey, streets of gold,
High walls of jasper . . . ' phrases rolled
Upon the tongues of idiots.
What profit *then,* if hunger gluts
Us *now?* Better my God should be
This moving, breathing frame of me,
Strong hands and feet, live heart and eyes;
And when these cease, say then God dies.
Your God is somewhere worlds away
Hunting a star He shot astray;
Oh, He has weightier things to do
Than lavish time on me and you.

What thought has He of us, three motes
Of breath, three scattered notes
In His grand symphony, the world?
Once we were blown, once we were hurled
In place, we were as soon forgot.
He might not linger on one dot
When there were bars and staves to fling
About, for waiting stars to sing.
When Rome was a suckling, when Greece
    was young,
Then there were Gods fit to be sung,
Who paid the loyal devotee
For service rendered zealously,
In coin a man might feel and spend,
Not marked 'Deferred to Journey's End.'
The servant then was worth his hire;
He went unscathed through flood and fire;
Gods were a thing then to admire.
'Bow down and worship us,' they said.
'You shall be clothed, be housed and fed,
While yet you live, not when you're dead.
Strong are our arms where yours are weak.
On them that harm you will we wreak
The vengeance of a God though they
Were Gods like us in every way.
Not merely is an honor laid
On those we touch with our accolade;

We strike for you with that same blade!' "
My mother shook a weary head—
"Visions are not for all," she said,
"There were no risings from the dead,
No frightened quiverings of earth
To mark my spirit's latter birth.
The light that on Damascus' road
Blinded a scoffer never glowed
For me. I had no need to view
His side, or pass my fingers through
Christ's wounds. It breaks like that on some,
And yet it can as surely come
Without the lightning and the rain.
Some who must have their hurricane
Go stumbling through it for a light
They never find. Only the night
Of doubt is opened to their sight.
They weigh and measure, search, define,—
But he who seeks a thing divine
Must humbly lay his lore aside,
And like a child believe; confide
In Him whose ways are deep and dark,
And in the end perhaps the spark
He sought will be revealed. Perchance
Some things are hard to countenance,
And others difficult to probe;
But shall the mind that grew this globe,

And out of chaos thought a world,
To us be totally unfurled?
And all we fail to comprehend,
Shall such a mind be asked to bend
Down to, unravel, and untwine?
If those who highest hold His sign,
Who praise Him most with loudest tongue
Are granted no high place among
The crowd, shall we be bitter then?
The puzzle shall grow simple when
The soul discards the ways of dust.
There is no gain in doubt; but trust
Is our one magic wand. Through it
We and eternity are knit,
Death made a myth, and darkness lit.
The slave can meet the monarch's gaze
With equal pride, dreaming to days
When slave and monarch both shall be,
Transmuted everlastingly,
A single reed blown on to sing
The glory of the only King."

We had not, in the stealthy gloom
Of deepening night, that shot our room
With queerly capering shadows through,
Noticed the form that wavered to
And fro on weak, unsteady feet

Within the door; I turned to greet
Spring's gayest cavalier, but Jim
Who stood there balanced in the dim
Half-light waved me away from him.
And then I saw how terror streaked
His eyes, and how a red flow leaked
And slid from cheek to chin. His hand
Still grasped a knotted branch, and spanned
It fiercely, fondling it. At last
He moved into the light, and cast
His eyes about, as if to wrap
In one soft glance, before the trap
Was sprung, all he saw mirrored there:
All love and bounty; grace; all fair,
All discontented days; sweet weather;
Rain-slant, snow-fall; all things together
Which any man about to die
Might ask to have filmed on his eye,
And then he bowed his haughty head,
"The thing we feared has come," he said;
"But put your ear down to the ground,
And you may hear the deadly sound
Of two-limbed dogs that bay for me.
If any ask in time to be
Why I was parted from my breath,
Here is your tale: I went to death
Because a man murdered the spring.

Tell them though they dispute this thing,
This is the song that dead men sing:
One spark of spirit God head gave
To all alike, to sire and slave,
From earth's red core to each white pole,
This one identity of soul;
That when the pipes of beauty play,
The feet must dance, the limbs must sway,
And even the heart with grief turned lead,
Beauty shall lift like a leaf wind-sped,
Shall swoop upon in gentle might,
Shall toss and tease and leave so light
That never again shall grief or care
Find long or willing lodgement there.
Tell them each law and rule they make
Mankind shall disregard and break
(If this must be) for beauty's sake.
Tell them what pranks the spring can play;
The young colt leaps, the cat that lay
In a sullen ball all winter long
Breaks like a kettle into song;
Waving it high like a limber flail,
The kitten worries his own brief tail;
While man and dog sniff the wind alike,
For the new smell hurts them like a spike
Of steel thrust quickly through the breast;
Earth heaves and groans with a sharp unrest.

The poet, though he sang of death,
Finds tunes for music in simple breath;
Even the old, the sleepy-eyed,
Are stirred to movement by the tide.
But oh, the young, the aging young,
Spring is a sweetmeat to our tongue;
Spring is the pean; we the choir;
Spring is the fuel; we the fire.
Tell them spring's feathery weight will jar,
Though it were iron, any bar
Upreared by men to keep apart
Two who when probed down to the heart
Speak each a common tongue. Tell them
Two met, each stooping to the hem
Of beauty passing by. Such awe
Grew on them hate began to thaw
And fear and dread to melt and run
Like ice laid siege to by the sun.
Say for a moment's misty space
These had forgotten hue and race;
Spring blew too loud and green a blast
For them to think on rank and caste.
The homage they both understood,
(Taught on a bloody Christless rood)
Due from his dark to her brighter blood,
In such an hour, at such a time,
When all their world was one clear rhyme,

He could not give, nor she exact.
This only was a glowing fact:
Spring in a green and golden gown,
And feathered feet, had come to town;
Spring in a rich habiliment
That shook the breath and woke the spent
And sleepy pulse to a dervish beat,

Spring had the world again at her feet.
Spring was a lady fair and rich,
And they were fired with the season's itch
To hold her train or stroke her hair
And tell her shyly they found her fair.
Spring was a voice so high and clear
It broke their hearts as they leaned to hear

In stream and grass and soft bird's-wing;
Spring was in them and they were spring.
Then say, a smudge across the day,
A bit of crass and filthy clay,
A blot of ink upon a white
Page in a book of gold; a tight
Curled worm hid in the festive rose,
A mind so foul it hurt your nose,
Came one of earth's serene elect,
His righteous being warped and flecked
With what his thoughts were: stench and
      smut. . . .
I had gone on unheeding but
He struck me down, he called her slut,
And black man's mistress, bawdy whore,
And such like names, and many more,—
(Christ, what has spring to answer for!)
I had gone on, I had been wise,
Knowing my value in those eyes
That seared me through and out and in,
Finding a thing to taunt and grin
At in my hair and hue. My right
I knew could not outweigh his might
Who had the law for satellite—
Only I turned to look at her,
The early spring's first worshiper,
(Spring, what have you to answer for?)

The blood had fled from either cheek
And from her lips; she could not speak,
But she could only stand and stare
And let her pain stab through the air.
I think a blow to heart or head
Had hurt her less than what he said.
A blow can be so quick and kind,
But words will feast upon the mind
And gnaw the heart down to a shred,
And leave you living, yet leave you dead.
If he had only tortured me,
I could have borne it valiantly.
The things he said in littleness
Were cheap, the blow he dealt me less,
Only they totalled more; he gagged
And bound a spirit there; he dragged
A sunlit gown of gold and green,—
(The season's first, first to be seen)
And feathered feet, and a plumèd hat,—
(First of the year to be wondered at)
Through muck and mire, and by the hair
He caught a lady rich and fair.
His vile and puny fingers churned
Our world about that sang and burned
A while as never world before.
He had unlatched an icy door,
And let the winter in once more.

93

To kill a man is a woeful thing,
But he who lays a hand on spring,
Clutches the first bird by its throat
And throttles it in the midst of a note;
Whose breath upon the leaf-proud tree
Turns all that wealth to penury;
Whose touch upon the first shy flower
Gives it a blight before its hour;
Whose craven face above a pool
That otherwise were clear and cool,
Transforms that running silver dream
Into a hot and sluggish stream
Thus better fit to countenance
His own corrupt unhealthy glance,
Of all men is most infamous;
His deed is rank and blasphemous.
The erstwhile warm, the short time sweet,
Spring now lay frozen at our feet.
Say then, why say nothing more
Except I had to close the door;
And this man's leer loomed in the way.
The air began to sting; then say
There was this branch; I struck; he fell;
There's holiday, I think, in hell."

Outside the night began to groan
As heavy feet crushed twig and stone

Beating a pathway to our door;
A thin noise first, and then a roar
More animal than human grew
Upon the air until we knew
No mercy could be in the sound.
"Quick, hide," I said. I glanced around;
But no abyss gaped in the ground.
But in the eyes of fear a twig
Will seem a tree, a straw as big
To him who drowns as any raft.
So being mad, being quite daft,
I shoved him in a closet set
Against the wall. This would but let
Him breathe two minutes more, or three,
Before they dragged him out to be
Queer fruit upon some outraged tree.
Our room was in a moment lit
With flaring brands; men crowded it—
Old men whose eyes were better sealed
In sleep; strong men with muscles steeled
Like rods, whose place was in the field;
Striplings like Jim with just a touch
Of down upon the chin; for such
More fitting a secluded hedge
To lie beneath with one to pledge
In youth's hot words, immortal love.
These things they were not thinking of;

"Lynch him! Lynch him!" O savage cry,
Why should you echo, "Crucify!"
One sought, sleek-tongued, to pacify
Them with slow talk of trial, law,
Established court; the dripping maw
Would not be wheedled from its prey.
Out of the past I heard him say,
"So be it then; have then your way;
But not by me shall blood be spilt;
I wash my hands clean of this guilt."
This was an echo of a phrase
Uttered how many million days
Gone by?

    Water may cleanse the hands
But what shall scour the soul that stands
Accused in heaven's sight?

               "The Kid."
One cried, "Where is the bastard hid?"
"He is not here."

          It was a faint
And futile lie.

        "The hell he ain't;
We tracked him here. Show us the place,
Or else . . ."

        He made an ugly face,
Raising a heavy club to smite.
I had been felled, had not the sight

Of all been otherwise arraigned.
Each with bewilderment unfeigned
Stared hard to see against the wall
The hunted boy stand slim and tall;
Dream-born, it seemed, with just a trace
Of weariness upon his face,
He stood as if evolved from air;
As if always he had stood there. . . .
What blew the torches' feeble flare
To such a soaring fury now?
Each hand went up to fend each brow,
Save his; he and the light were one,
A man by night clad with the sun.
By form and feature, bearing, name,
I knew this man. He was the same
Whom I had thrust, a minute past,
Behind a door,—and made it fast.
Knit flesh and bone, had like a thong,
Bound us as one our whole life long,
But in the presence of this throng,
He seemed one I had never known.
Never such tragic beauty shone
As this on any face before.
It pared the heart straight to the core.
It is the lustre dying lends,
I thought, to make some brief amends
To life so wantonly cut down.

The air about him shaped a crown
Of light, or so it seemed to me,
And sweeter than the melody
Of leaves in rain, and far more sad,
His voice descended on the mad,
Blood-sniffing crowd that sought his life,
A voice where grief cut like a knife:
"I am he whom you seek, he whom
You will not spare his daily doom.
My march is ever to the tomb,
But let the innocent go free;
This man and woman, let them be,
Who loving much have succored me."
And then he turned about to speak
To me whose heart was fit to break,
"My brother, when this wound has healed,
And you reap in some other field
Roses, and all a spring can yield;
Brother (to call me so!) then prove
Out of your charity and love
That I was not unduly slain,
That this my death was not in vain.
For no life should go to the tomb
Unless from it a new life bloom,
A greater faith, a clearer sight,
A wiser groping for the light."
He moved to where our mother stood,

Dry-eyed, though grief was at its flood,
"Mother, not poorer losing one,
Look now upon your dying son."
Her own life trembling on the brim,
She raised woe-ravaged eyes to him,
And in their glances something grew
And spread, till healing fluttered through
Her pain, a vision so complete
It sent her humbly to his feet
With what I deemed a curious cry,
"And must this be for such as I?"
Even his captors seemed to feel
Disquietude, an unrest steal
Upon their ardor, dampening it,
Till one less fearful varlet hit
Him across the mouth a heavy blow,
Drawing a thin, yet steady flow
Of red to drip a dirge of slow
Finality upon my heart.
The end came fast. Given the start
One hound must always give the pack
That fears the meekest prey whose back
Is desperate against a wall,
They charged. I saw him stagger, fall
Beneath a mill of hands, feet, staves.
And I like one who sees huge waves
In hunger rise above the skiff

At sea, yet watching from a cliff
Far off can lend no feeblest aid,
No more than can a fragile blade
Of grass in some far distant land,
That has no heart to wrench, nor hand
To stretch in vain, could only stand
With streaming eyes and watch the play.

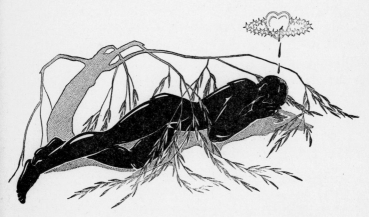

There grew a tree a little way
Off from the hut, a virgin tree
Awaiting its fecundity.
O Tree was ever worthier Groom
Led to a bride of such rare bloom?
Did ever fiercer hands enlace
Love and Beloved in an embrace
As heaven-smiled-upon as this?

Was ever more celestial kiss?
But once, did ever anywhere
So full a choir chant such an air
As feathered splendors bugled there?
And was there ever blinder eye
Or deafer ear than mine?

                              A cry
So soft, and yet so brimming filled
With agony, my heart strings thrilled
An ineffectual reply,—
Then gaunt against the southern sky
The silent handiwork of hate.
Greet, Virgin Tree, your holy mate!

No sound then in the little room
Was filtered through my sieve of gloom,
Except the steady fall of tears,
The hot, insistent rain that sears
The burning ruts down which it goes,
The futile flow, for all one knows
How vain it is, that ever flows.
I could not bear to look at *her*
There in the dark; I could not stir
From where I sat, so weighted down.
The king of grief, I held my crown
So dear, I wore my tattered gown
With such affection and such love

That though I strove I could not move.
But I could hear (and this unchained
The raging beast in me) her pained
And sorrow-riven voice ring out
Above the spirit's awful rout,
Above the howling winds of doubt,
How she knew Whom she traveled to
Was judge of all that men might do
To such as she who trusted Him.
Faith was a tower for her, grim
And insurmountable; and death
She said was only changing breath
Into an essence fine and rare.
Anger smote me and most despair
Seeing her still bow down in prayer.
"Call on Him now," I mocked, "and try
Your faith against His deed, while I
With intent equally as sane,
Searching a motive for this pain,
Will hold a little stone on high
And seek of it the reason why.
Which, stone or God, will first reply?
Why? Hear me ask it. He was young
And beautiful. Why was he flung
Like common dirt to death? Why, stone,
Must he of all the earth atone
For what? The dirt God used was homely

But the man He made was comely.
What child creating out of sand,
With puckered brow and intent hand,
Would see the lovely thing he planned
Struck with a lewd and wanton blade,

Nor stretch a hand to what he made,
Nor shed a childish, futile tear,
Because he loved it, held it dear?
Would not a child's weak heart rebel?
But Christ who conquered Death and Hell

What has He done for you who spent
A bleeding life for His content?
Or is the white Christ, too, distraught
By these dark sins His Father wrought?"

I mocked her so until I broke
Beneath my passion's heavy yoke.
My world went black with grief and pain;
My very bitterness was slain,
And I had need of only sleep,
Or some dim place where I might weep
My life away, some misty haunt
Where never man might come to taunt
Me with the thought of how men scar
Their brothers here, or what we are
Upon this most accursèd star.
Not that sweet sleep from which some wake
All fetterless, without an ache
Of heart or limb, but such a sleep
As had raped him, eternal, deep;—
Deep as my woe, vast as my pain,
Sleep of the young and early-slain.
My Lycidas was dead. There swung
In all his glory, lusty, young,
My Jonathan, my Patrocles,
(For with his death there perished these)
And I had neither sword nor song,

Only an acid-bitten tongue,
Fit neither in its poverty
For vengeance nor for threnody,
Only for tears and blasphemy.

Now God be praised that a door should creak,
And that a rusty hinge should shriek.
Of all sweet sounds that I may hear
Of lute or lyre or dulcimer,
None ever shall assail my ear
Sweet as the sound of a grating door
I had thought closed forevermore.
Out of my deep-ploughed agony,
I turned to see a door swing free;
The very door he once came through
To death, now framed for us anew
His vital self, his and no other's
Live body of the dead, my brother's.
Like one who dreams within a dream,
Hand at my throat, lest I should scream,
I moved with hopeful, doubting pace
To meet the dead man face to face.

"Bear witness now unto His grace";
I heard my mother's mounting word,
"Behold the glory of the Lord,
His unimpeachable high seal.

Cry mercy now before Him; kneel,
And let your heart's conversion swell
The wonder of His miracle."

I saw; I touched; yet doubted him;
My fingers faltered down his slim
Sides, down his breathing length of limb.
Incredulous of sight and touch,
"No more," I cried, "this is too much
For one mad brain to stagger through."
For there he stood in utmost view
Whose death I had been witness to;
But now he breathed; he lived; he walked;
His tongue could speak my name; he talked.
He questioned me to know what art
Had made his enemies depart.
Either I leaped or crawled to where
I last had seen stiff on the air
The form than life more dear to me;
But where had swayed that misery
Now only was a flowering tree
That soon would travail into fruit.
Slowly my mind released its mute
Bewilderment, while truth took root
In me and blossomed into light:
"Down, down," I cried, in joy and fright,
As all He said came back to me

With what its true import must be,
"Upon our knees and let the worst,
Let me the sinfullest kneel first;
O lovely Head to dust brought low
More times than we can ever know
Whose small regard, dust-ridden eye,
Behold Your doom, yet doubt You die;
O Form immaculately born,
Betrayed a thousand times each morn,
As many times each night denied,
Surrendered, tortured, crucified!
Now have we seen beyond degree
That love which has no boundary;
Our eyes have looked on Calvary."

No sound then in the sacred gloom
That blessed the shrine that was our room
Except the steady rise of praise
To Him who shapes all nights and days
Into one final burst of sun;
Though with the praise some tears must run
In pity of the King's dear breath
That ransomed one of us from death.

The days are mellow for us now;
We reap full fields; the heavy bough

Bends to us in another land;
The ripe fruit falls into our hand.
My mother, Job's dark sister, sits
Now in a corner, prays, and knits.
Often across her face there flits
Remembered pain, to mar her joy,
At Whose death gave her back her boy.
While I who mouthed my blasphemies,
Recalling now His agonies,
Am found forever on my knees,
Ever to praise her Christ with her,
Knowing He can at will confer
Magic on miracle to prove
And try me when I doubt His love.
If I am blind He does not see;
If I am lame He halts with me;
There is no hood of pain I wear
That has not rested on His hair
Making Him first initiate
Beneath its harsh and hairy weight.
He grew with me within the womb;
He will receive me at the tomb.
He will make plain the misty path
He makes me tread in love and wrath,
And bending down in peace and grace
May wear again my brother's face.

Somewhere the Southland rears a tree,
(And many others there may be
Like unto it, that are unknown,
Whereon as costly fruit has grown).
It stands before a hut of wood
In which the Christ Himself once stood—
And those who pass it by may see
Nought growing there except a tree,
But there are two to testify
Who hung on it . . . we saw Him die.
Its roots were fed with priceless blood.
It is the Cross; it is the Rood.

Paris, January 31, 1929.